The Original Snow Village©

1976 ~ 1990

Collectors' Album

TEXT BY JAMES P. WICKESBERG

Department 56

How the Collectors' Album was organized...

The first and perhaps most important issue facing Department 56 in compiling a complete history of The Original Snow Village© was how to represent an accurate, chronological grouping of the pieces each year from 1976 to the present. The only way to arrive at such a grouping was to list pieces according to a standard that would remain consistent throughout the years, and it was decided that pieces would be best categorized according to their year of introduction. This information is contained in the bottom-stamps of most Original Snow Village pieces, with the exception of models from the earliest years. Although it is not meant to be confusing, this method of grouping the pieces has puzzled a number of collectors, who logically assume that the year of introduction reflects the first year in which a piece is made available to the collector. In reality, however, because Department 56 must develop designs at least one year in advance, the year of introduction for any given piece must reflect the first year in which a piece is designed, sculpted and copyrighted. In most cases, the piece is not available to the collector until the following year, when Department 56 is able to distribute the latest Original Snow Village designs to the retailers, or dealers. For example, the Toy Shop (#5073-3) was designed, sculpted and copyrighted in 1986, so the year of introduction for the Toy Shop will be 1986, but the piece was not available to collectors until 1987. As we follow the history of The Original Snow Village, pieces will be dated according to their year of introduction as described above. A complete chronological listing of all designs can be found beginning on page 99.

The Original Snow Village©
1976 ~ 1990

Our special thanks to
Ed and Jean Rahn and Lorena Lane
for lending us their pieces to make our Collectors' Album complete.

Just imagine…snow-laden trees, wreaths at the windows and welcome mats out…
Since 1976, these words have come to represent the charming period buildings and soft glowing lights of The Original Snow Village© by Department 56.

There are special traditions for each of us in which our most treasured holiday memories are kept alive. As the season draws near, we can search through old bits of faded tinsel, or stiff strings of dusty lights and suddenly, magically, we are gazing through a frosty wreath at grandmother's window or wandering the snow-covered streets of our own home town. Year after year, the magic of the holiday season rekindles these cherished memories, and we preserve them in beloved traditions that will never be forgotten or outgrown.

Over the past 14 years, The Original Snow Village has become one of these special traditions, sparking our imaginations with nostalgic images that recall the joy and warmth of the holiday season.

This year, once again, "the tradition continues…"

IN THE BEGINNING…

On a holiday outing many years ago, a group of friends planned to enjoy Christmas dinner at a small country inn located in a quiet little town on the St. Croix River. The journey to the inn was delightful, as everyone recalled childhood memories, family traditions and the images that personally inspired the joy of the season for one and all. Frosty farmland, peaceful churches, bustling shops and warm, bright houses passed by while the group drove merrily through the snow-covered countryside.

Suddenly, as they rounded a bend in the road, conversation stopped. Spread out before them was a small, turn-of-the-century village, decorated for the holidays and gently covered with new-fallen snow. Shop windows beamed, a church bell rang, and smoke curled up from the snowy Town Hall chimney. There was a bakery, a toy store, a fire station and an old-fashioned schoolhouse, all trimmed with bright, glistening icicles.

A variety of well-kept Victorian, Federal, and Colonial homes lined the streets, each with fresh wreaths at the windows and lights cheerfully aglow. At the end of the street, the tall spire of a clapboard church looked down on a group of friendly carolers singing near a holly-covered lamppost. The setting was so heartwarming, everyone knew that this evening would be a cherished memory forever.

An idea occurred that night...to recreate the charming little village and the feelings it inspired, scaling it down so that it could exist for everyone, everywhere. That idea became a reality early in 1976 when Department 56 introduced The Original Snow Village, a series of six handpainted ceramic buildings which included four houses and two small churches. Since then, The Original Snow Village has grown to include 128 lit houses, shops, churches and a variety of other lighted pieces. In addition, a large number of non-lit ceramic and metal accessories have been added over the years to enhance the village settings.

Traditionally, several pieces are retired from the collection each year as newer designs are introduced. The new designs assure that The Original Snow Village will steadily continue to grow, and retiring older pieces limits the number of pieces produced in any given design.

In this collector's volume, we are pleased to offer you the complete story of The Original Snow Village, from the idea stage all the way through design, manufacturing and packaging. We also include a comprehensive history and full-color photographs, followed by a complete listing of every lit piece and accessory in The Original Snow Village Collection.

Manufacturing

BUILDING A SNOW HOUSE...

Each charming piece of miniature real estate in The Original Snow Village Collection is the final product of an intricate and lengthy "construction" process. Every design starts out as a very simple idea, but before it can be delivered to you, the collector, it goes through various stages of drawing, sculpting, bottom-stamping, molding, casting, firing, hand painting, and packaging. The following pages offer a detailed outline of the steps that go into "building" a Snow House.

THE IDEA...

In the early years of The Original Snow Village, building designs came from a number of sources. American artists and overseas craftsmen put their imaginations to work creating the charmingly diverse pieces that became the valuable cornerstones of today's ongoing collection. More recently, new Snow Village pieces have been designed almost exclusively by the Department 56 creative staff, with imaginative input from collectors, dealers and friends around the world.

DRAWINGS...

For each original design, scaled drawings are created which become the "blueprints" for a new Snow Village building. Front, side and rear elevations indicate exactly what each side of the building will look like, including all exterior details. Windows, doors, shutters, awnings, porches, pillars, gables, dormers, chimneys, clapboard and brick must all be drawn in exact proportion. A roof plan is drawn to indicate peaks, points, and shingles. Finally, a "colorbreak" is laid over the drawing to indicate the proposed colors of all facings and trim. When properly done, the drawings will act as a detailed guide for the sculptor who will transform the drawings into a three-dimensional representation.

SCULPTING...

Snow Village pieces take shape beginning with a clay model known as a "prototype." The sculpting of each building is a complicated, meticulous process which can last for several days. As a building is sculpted, the sculptor must keep in mind that the clay model is made 5% larger than the desired final product size to offset shrinkage during kiln firing. The main body of the house is always sculpted first, followed by the detailing of each individual brick, board, and snow drift.

ATTACHMENTS...

Most details which extend beyond the flat surface of a building wall, such as chimneys, porches, pillars, dormers, and towers, must be individually sculpted. This requires extreme precision because the separate pieces will be "attached" at a later stage of production, and they must fit perfectly without unsightly markings or gaps. If an attachment is well executed, it takes a sharp eye to determine where it is joined to the main body.

An Original Snow Village piece begins to take shape as the sculptor carefully transforms an artist's rendering into a clay prototype which will be used to create the mother molds.

Attachments, like this church tower, must fit perfectly. They are "glued" into place using a mixture of clay slip just before the piece is sent to the kiln for firing.

BOTTOM-STAMPING...

During the sculpting stage, a "bottom-stamp" is prepared which contains specific information pertaining to the design that will be embossed on the bottom of the piece. Over the years, these bottom-stamps have undergone a process of evolution, so it is often possible to determine the approximate age of a particular piece by the type of bottom-stamp which appears (or does not appear) on the underside of the piece.

When The Original Snow Village began (1976-1980), it was never expected that one day it would become a sought-after collectible. Because of this,

pieces from the early years often display little or no information on the bottom. Craftsmen from different local areas had different ways of hand-marking pieces, while some put in no marks at all. These regional differences account for a wide range of variations found on the pieces through the years and are still a factor today.

From approximately 1978-1986, if bottom-stamps appeared they were usually carved in the bottom of the piece by hand. These "stamps" most often included the name of the piece and a Department 56 copyright, usually abbreviated as

The information displayed on early Snow Village models was always hand carved, usually brief, and in many cases non-existent.

One of the drawbacks of hand carved bottom-stamps was that occasionally a craftsman might add a unique (but confusing) touch, as in the example above, picturing the 1985 Depot and Train!

© Dept. 56. Later years also included the year of original design. As The Original Snow Village grew, an effort was made to provide meaningful information for an expanding group of appreciative collectors.

From 1986-1988, the increased demand for accurate marking of Snow Village pieces prompted the development of a more comprehensive bottom-stamp. The first marking to be incorporated into the molds was the Department 56 copyright logo. Many pieces from these years display a combination of this molded stamp and handcarved markings. With rare exception, each piece now displays the design title, year of original design, The Original Snow Village logo, and the Department 56 copyright symbol. These markings are permanently contained in the mold and indicate a genuine Original Snow Village collectible.

After 1986, most models displayed a bottom-stamp that was sculpted or stamped directly in the mold so that all pieces of a given design carried consistent information.

All bottom-stamps now display the design name, year of introduction, The Original Snow Village logo and the Department 56 copyright symbol.

Production molds often consist of up to six parts which must be fit tightly together before the casting process begins.

A liquid clay mixture known as "slip" is hand-poured into the production mold. The porous mold will absorb some of the moisture from the clay as the piece begins to harden.

Because the molds used in production are light-weight and porous, they eventually "wear out". After 30-40 castings, a production mold must be dismantled and destroyed.

MOLD MAKING...

From the finely detailed clay sculpture and bottom-stamp, a mold impression is taken using a specially formulated super-fine plaster. This first mold is called the "mother mold." Through a series of complex processes, requiring a high level of technical skill, the mother mold is transformed into what is known as a "case mold," sometimes referred to as a "master mold." An extra hard, high density composite is used to form the case mold, thus preserving sharp details during repeated usage.

"Production molds," made of highly porous plaster mixture, are in turn produced from the case molds. The plaster mixture will absorb some of the moisture contained in the liquid clay that is poured in the mold to form the final piece. The production molds are separated into as many as six parts which are banded tightly together before the casting process begins. Unlike the case molds, the production molds are porous and lightweight, hence they will wear out after 30-40 castings. Depending on the quantities ordered, up to several hundred production molds may be required for a given design in order to maintain a high degree of sharpness and detail. Once a production mold is no longer usable, it is broken and discarded; when a design is finally retired, the case molds are also destroyed.

The liquid slip is sometimes "injected" into the production molds, which are securely banded together to prevent the clay mixture from escaping.

Excess slip is slowly drained off of the molds as they are left idle to allow the clay bodies to harden. When the molds are unbanded, a semi-firm clay structure will emerge.

Door and window openings are hand-cut while the clay is still relatively soft. Each opening requires 4-6 separate hand-cuts.

CASTING...

Slip casting is the first step in the actual production of an Original Snow Village piece. Liquid clay, or "slip," is poured into the cavity of the production mold. Moisture is drawn out of the clay slip and into the porous plaster mold, forming a thin wall of drier clay along the inside of the mold cavity. Excess slip is poured out, and the mold is left idle to allow the clay body to harden. Finally, the mold is unbanded and the parts carefully removed, leaving a hollow, semi-firm clay structure.

Adjustments to the clay body are necessary before the piece is ready for kiln firing. Mold lines are gently sanded and sponged away, and at this time the attachments are carefully "glued" into place using a clay slip mixture.

Before the pieces are fired, the window and door openings are hand-cut to let out the soft, glowing light that has made The Original Snow Village famous. An individual design may have as many as 50 window openings, each requiring 4-6 separate hand-cuts, for a total of over 200 cuts per piece! After the cuts are made, the pieces are set out to dry for up to 24 hours before they are loaded into the kiln.

FIRING...

Kiln firing is the final step in preparation of the ceramic body. The unfired clay bodies are placed on shelves in a "box," or "periodic" kiln. These kilns average 78 cubic ft. in volume, and can fire up to 450 Snow Village houses in one firing. Once the kiln is loaded and sealed, it is slowly heated over a period of eight hours until the temperature climbs to 980°F., where it remains for approximately ½ hour. The kiln is then turned off and allowed to slowly cool for up to five hours. This prevents cracking and warping of the ceramic bodies.

HANDPAINTING AND GLAZING...

Handpainting, by far the most time-consuming stage of production, is executed by highly skilled artisans whose talents include patience and extreme concentration. The various colors are applied directly to the fired clay buildings with large brushes using oil-base epoxy paints. Finer details such as windows, shutters, doors and signs are then painted using smaller brushes, taking care not to overlap colors. Finally, the drifts of snow are applied over the painted roofs and doorways. The completed houses are then baked in a "low fire" electric oven at 150°F., permanently bonding the paint and snow to the ceramic surface.

The clay bodies are stacked on shelves and loaded into large box kilns which can fire up to 450 pieces at a time. After the 15-hour firing process, the pieces are ready for handpainting or glazing.

Some designs require a clear glaze to be applied in a second firing. The glazed bodies are then handpainted and baked a third time to bond the paint to the glazed ceramic surface. The finished product is shown above.

Designs whose color schemes include white are glazed before they are handpainted. This treatment allows the natural ceramic color to show through in areas which are not covered by paint. The fired ceramic piece is dipped into a clear liquid glaze and then fired a second time, requiring an additional eight hours, with final temperatures reaching up to 1080°F. After glazing, the paint and snow are then applied in the same manner as on the unglazed pieces, then baked in the electric oven prior to packaging.

The patience and skilled concentration of the Snow Village painters is apparent in every piece, from the foundation to the brightly colored roof. Many designs include hand-lettered signs.

As the designs are handpainted, the bottom-stamps are inspected, and window openings are checked to make sure the piece is ready for packaging.

Glazing a piece allows the natural "white" ceramic color to show through in areas which will not be covered by paint. The pieces on the right have been glazed only, while those on the left are complete.

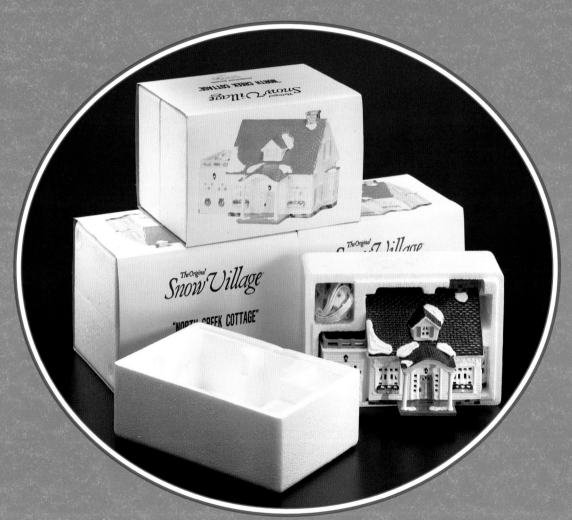

PACKAGING...

Once a piece is fully "constructed," it is carefully cleaned and packed securely in an individual storage carton, complete with illustrated sleeve and a special compartment containing the UL approved switched cord and bulb. This sturdy, attractive packaging has been developed over the last several years to replace the disposable boxes that were still being used as recently as 1985. The new packaging better protects the pieces during shipping, and provides a convenient method of repacking so that your collection can be safely stored for many years to come.

After years of development, the packaging of The Original Snow Village pieces now includes attractive, illustrated sleeves and individually molded storage cartons.

1976

J ust imagine...long, long ago, in a quiet, friendly little river valley, someplace on the edge of a bright, snowy Somewhere...the first humble foundations of The Original Snow Village took shape. Nestled peacefully among gently rolling hills and tall, frosty evergreens were six simple structures: the Mountain Lodge, the Gabled Cottage, The Inn, the Country Church, the Steepled Church and the Small Chalet.

The charming appeal of these early buildings lay in their somewhat rough construction and bright, colorful painting, both distinctive features of this first era in Snow Village history. Like most pioneer homes and churches, these simple designs displayed a unique character which has continued to distinguish them from any of the buildings which eventually followed.

Although these early pieces were not complex, the painted details added touches that individually defined each building. The creeping vines and quaint, hand-lettered messages on the Country Church, or the gaily colored skis and cheerful sunburst on the Mountain Lodge were characteristic of this painting style. Each of the original pieces displayed a warm, wholesome quality, from the ivy-colored walls of the Gabled Cottage to the stout brick chimneys of The Inn.

The initial introductions were inspired by simple, historic village scenes from around the world. These six landmark buildings were the first pieces to represent the basic elements around which The Original Snow Village would grow and prosper, namely, the universal warmth and nostalgic spirit which inspire our fondest holiday memories. As we follow this history through the years, we continue to look back on these original buildings with pride as the foundations of a new tradition. Welcome to The Original Snow Village!

THE COMPLETE 1976 ORIGINAL SNOW VILLAGE© COLLECTION

The six 1976 designs shown here represent the beginning of The Original Snow Village tradition. In the following pages, one chapter is devoted to each year in the development of the Snow Village. Entire village scenes will be pictured that feature all designs available in a given year, including those designs carried over from previous years. All designs newly introduced in a given year will be pictured separately in the chapter corresponding to their year of introduction.

Historical Footnote: The Gabled Cottage and The Inn were the first Snow Village designs to actually put the "famous" Snow Village welcome mats out!

Steepled Church (1976-1979): A single spire rose from the Steepled Church, where old iron church bells would have rung out news of a wedding or holiday.

The Inn (1976-1979): If holiday guests made the magical journey to the Snow Village but couldn't bring themselves to leave, The Inn was a good place to stay.

Country Church (1976-1979): This classic example of early Snow Village charm displayed its warm, hand painted welcome on walls shaded by an original snow-laden tree.

Small Chalet (1976-1979): Looking just as if it were constructed of thick, rich gingerbread, the Small Chalet was the simplest design ever imagined in the Snow Village.

Mountain Lodge (1976-1979): The Lodge featured the colorful hand painting and simple, handcrafted look that was characteristic of the six original designs.

Gabled Cottage (1976-1979): Charming curtained windows, ivied walls and an original welcome mat made visitors to the Gabled Cottage feel right at home.

Several interpretations of The Original Snow Village welcome mats appear on designs throughout the years, none more charming than the first version, pictured above.

The Snow Village community didn't change much during the first year. The six houses and churches of The Original Snow Village continued to shed their welcoming light among the silent, snow-laden trees. But…on the outskirts of town…

The Victorian House, the Mansion and the Stone Church, all introduced in 1977, altered the landscape of the Snow Village forever. These three new pieces were an interesting and dramatic change in design from the six original buildings. Borrowing from a broader range of traditional architectural styles, the new houses and church moved away from the simple country village style of the initial introductions. New "building" materials were revealed in the sculpting of the textured pink shingles and neat clapboard on the Victorian House, the sturdy, white brick facade of the Mansion, and the chiseled limestone of the Stone Church.

This year, and in the many years to come, as the detailing and the style of the village developed, so did the scope of our imaginations. Instead of just a charming holiday decoration on the mantel or under the tree, The Original Snow Village was becoming a "place"…a place to experience the warmth of the holidays, past, present and future. It was a place with something to offer everyone, whether it was a gift of cherished memories, the opportunity to appreciate the special joy of the season, or just a simple daydream of tomorrow.

This special quality, coupled with the offering of new designs in 1977 gave the earliest indication that The Original Snow Village might be developing as an ongoing series. In their own unique manner, the three new buildings enhanced the warm spirit and nostalgic charm of the entire collection, which now boasted a total of nine pieces!

Stone Church (1977-1979): Its snow-laden tree and colorful exterior made it obvious that this early Norman-style church was built on native Snow Village soil.

Victorian House (1977-1979): At the Victorian House, tea was served every day after the stained glass was clean and the front steps were swept clear of new-fallen snow.

THE COMPLETE 1977 ORIGINAL SNOW VILLAGE© COLLECTION

All three of the 1977 introductions, and many of the pieces that followed, featured an attached "snow-laden" evergreen tree, similar to the six original designs. A single lit house with an attached tree, also lit, often made these designs appear to be two pieces. To create this effect, a small opening was formed where the ceramic tree was joined to the main house body, allowing light to be transmitted directly from the house to the tree. Both "pieces" were illuminated using a single bulb.

Mansion (1977-1979): The Mansion had shuttered windows, brick walls and a square cupola, details which would have been unimaginable in 1976.

1978

With friendly foundations securely in place, an established mixture of charming, traditional architecture, and the potential of a continuing collection, The Original Snow Village was ready to grow. In 1978, six new pieces were introduced: the Homestead, the General Store, the Cape Cod, the Nantucket, the Skating Rink/Duck Pond Set and Small Double Trees. Although many new ideas and a variety of delightful, appealing additions would be offered in the coming years, the 1978 pieces retain a special place in Snow Village History.

For the first time, the new designs reflected a distinctly regional influence. The New England style was reminiscent of many small towns throughout eastern America. In the Snow Village, as in many early settlements, the General Store became the first merchant establishment, offering the small community everything from postal service to a gallon of gas. The list of charming houses "constructed" this year featured two of the longest running designs in Snow Village History. The Homestead, available for six years, was surpassed only by the Nantucket, which ran for eight years and became the most popular house design ever introduced.

The Skating Rink/Duck Pond Set and Small Double Trees represented the first introduction of non-house accessory pieces to the Snow Village. These new pieces made history because they allowed our imaginations to expand the village setting out beyond our welcome mats and the wreaths at our windows. Most importantly, the accessories could strengthen the enchantment of the Snow Village magic, whether they were accompanied by just one single house or by all thirteen of the lighted buildings available thus far. Though safe and warm in our own homes, we could lace up our old skates or sit gingerly on the edge of an icy bench, listening to the cold winter quiet beneath huge, snow-laden trees.

Through the years, Department 56 has proudly maintained a collection of every Original Snow Village piece ever produced. Just imagine our surprise when an inventory of our collection revealed that two of our pieces were badly damaged! The picture of the Cape Cod house on this page and the picture of the Parish Church, 1984 (pg. 52), were made possible by generous, trusting collectors who sent us their pieces to be photographed.

 **Historical Footnote:** The Skating Rink/Duck Pond Set was destined for early retirement. The heavy, snow laden trees were attached directly to the flat "pond" bases, and their size and weight caused frequent breakage. The set was retired the following year, but popular demand for the pieces caused a revised version, the Skating Pond, to be introduced in 1982. At that time, the trees were molded separately.

Nantucket (1978-1986): Everyone imagines living in a charming little cottage by the sea, which explains why Nantucket became the most popular, longest running design ever introduced.

Skating Rink/Duck Pond Set (1978-1979): A friendly snowman and icy woodpile helped these first non-house pieces to create an old-fashioned feeling of the great outdoors.

Cape Cod (1978-1980): The Cape Cod's traditional features included a central chimney, steep gabled roof, half-story dormer and complete landscaping!

General Store (1978-1980): In 1978, the General Store introduced postal service, a gas pump and a small-town landmark to the growing Snow Village community.

Homestead (1978-1984): Big old farmhouses like this were once part of the American dream. Snow Village dreams are created by a fertile imagination.

For three years, the quiet, old-fashioned river town that inspired The Original Snow Village had been captured in quaint, modest buildings that reflected the integrity and charm of a simpler time. To get there, one had only to add a dash of imagination to a pinch of holiday spirit, and mix with a trace of well-seasoned memory. But imagination and memory serve each of us differently. We all have our individual potpourri of holiday images that inspire in us the joys of the season, past and present. The feelings experienced are similar for everyone, but the inspiration is rarely the same. What this suggested for The Original Snow Village was diversity.

In 1979, the Snow Village expanded with the largest number of new introductions in its four year history. Additions included the Victorian, Knob Hill, Brownstone, Log Cabin, Countryside Church, Stone Church, School House, Tudor House, Mission Church, Giant Trees, and the Carolers accessory group. Almost every style of building imaginable turned up somewhere in the Snow Village this year, including the Adobe House and the Mobile Home.

The year 1979 is most notable in Snow Village history as the first year in which previous Snow Village designs were retired. All six of the original 1976 buildings, the three additional 1977 models and the 1978 Skating Rink/Duck Pond Set were retired to accommodate the large and varied assortment of new pieces introduced in 1979.

The decision to retire a design is always carefully considered, and most often based on factors unrelated to the popularity of a piece. Usually there will be production matters to consider that render it impossible to faithfully reproduce a given design, even if it is a favorite, and the piece will be retired. In some cases, after a piece has enjoyed a long and successful run, it will be retired to limit the number of pieces produced and to allow new designs to prosper in the tradition of the ever-changing Snow Village.

Victorian (1979-1982): From terrace to turret, the cheerful glow of the red-roofed, clapboard Victorian was a charming addition to any Snow Village street.

Stone Church (1979-1980): For those who missed the original 1977-1979 Stone Church, this large but familiar-looking design was heaven-sent.

Brownstone (1979-1981): When the occupants of the Brownstone "just imagined" wreaths at their windows, eight wreaths appeared on the elegant front bays!

Once a design is retired, no additional pieces may be manufactured. Those models that are available for many years are produced in far greater quantities than those that are retired after only a year or two, making the latter among the rarest traces of Snow Village history. For example, the Mobile Home, pictured on this page, was one of the more unusual Snow Village designs. Retired after just two years due to production problems, it is now a hard-to-find collector's piece.

This year also marks the first appearance of Snow Village natives on the snow-covered streets. The three-piece Carolers set, the first non-lit accessory group to be introduced, featured Christmas carolers singing beneath a lamppost gaily decked with boughs of holly. This cheerful group recreated the scene that had so enchanted the holiday travellers years earlier when The Original Snow Village was just the beginning of a good idea.

Log Cabin (1979-1981): A pair of bright red skis waited on the front porch at the rustic Log Cabin, ready to make fresh tracks through the new-fallen snow.

School House (1979-1982): There are few nostalgic images as rich in memory as the one-room, red brick schoolhouse, a classic reminder of days gone by.

Mobile Home (1979-1980): Starting in 1979, you could take the Mobile Home out of the Snow Village, but you couldn't take the Snow Village out of the Mobile Home.

THE COMPLETE 1979 ORIGINAL SNOW VILLAGE© COLLECTION

Knob Hill (1979-1981): Many people left their hearts in the Snow Village because of this three-story San Francisco-style Victorian rowhouse.

Adobe House (1979-1980): At the Adobe House, the chile peppers hung from the timbers with care, in hopes that San Nicolas soon would be there.

Mission Church (1979-1980): The thick walls and brushed, sun-dried clay common to adobe style architecture gave the Mission Church a simple, Southwestern look.

Countryside Church (1979-1984): Famous for its rare variety of snow-laden tree, this church rang its chimes over the quiet, snow-covered countryside for six years.

Giant Trees (1979-1982): A mature form of the typical snow-laden variety, these over-sized arbors soon became an endangered species, retired after only four years.

Tudor House (1979-1981): A simple house reminiscent of the English countryside, this design featured timbered exterior walls and a split-shingle roof.

I n 1980, an approaching train whistled its greeting to The Original Snow Village. One of the only Snow Village models ever to be produced in Japan, the Train Station with Three Train Cars, a set of four individually lit pieces, seemed in some special way to complete the setting of the old-fashioned township unlike any other introduction to date. Whether it was the rich, colorful history associated with the railroad, or because it symbolized nostalgic holiday expeditions, the Train and Station offered an enduring image of romance. As a part of The Original Snow Village, the Train became a vehicle for our imaginary journeys, where travel was limited only by the boundaries of our dreams.

The other five 1980 introductions were a charming assortment of country-style buildings and churches. The domed and turreted Cathedral Church and the rustic Stone Mill House demonstrated the growing skill of Snow Village artisans. The simple Colonial Farm House and Town Church together with the Ceramic Car accessory completed the year's offerings. This was a relatively sparse offering due to the large number of continuing models from the previous year, and the few pieces that were retired at this time.

With the wide variety of Snow Village designs that had become available since 1976, an increasing number of people were finding themselves with a "collection". Whether it was two pieces or thirty-two, setting up the village every year was becoming as important as making the plum pudding or decorating the tree. What mattered most was not the number of pieces in a collection, but the special feeling that came from making the magical holiday journey into The Original Snow Village. It was a feeling of warmth, of memory. It was the feeling of tradition.

Train Station with Three Cars (1980-1985): This nostalgic, four-piece lighted set waited to magically transport imaginative holiday visitors on a moment's notice.

By 1981, the simple, old-fashioned buildings and soft, beaming lights of The Original Snow Village had captured many hearts and imaginations with their unique holiday charm. Those who had carefully placed a single piece on the mantel found that its cheerful glow invited and encouraged them to enjoy the warmth and excitement of the holiday season. In time, as other favorite pieces were added, it became an opportunity to build a tradition which could be appreciated by young and old alike for years to come. In its sixth year, The Original Snow Village was modestly taking its place as an ongoing collectible series.

The introductions this year included a broad range of interesting new city and country designs, evidence that the growing Snow Village was becoming something more than just a larger group of charming, but unrelated pieces. The community was beginning to reflect a simple bit of planning. The charmingly sculpted Barn was added in 1981 to compliment the Colonial Farm House, introduced the year before, while the red-bricked Corner Store and the clean, white Bakery became companions or replacements for the General Store, retired in 1980. Other additions offered a pleasant mixture of country color and city style, from the lovely thatched roof of the English Cottage to the porches of the traditional Wooden Clapboard. There were a total of eight new designs offered in 1981, including the timbered English Church, a snow-laden Large Single Tree and the Ceramic Sleigh, loaded with bright packages and a tree. These were eight small chapters in Snow Village History, eight new members of the community ready to welcome anyone with a bold imagination to the magic of The Original Snow Village.

Bakery (1981-1983): Nostalgia might be defined as the feeling which results from remembering that there really was a time when fresh, homemade pies could be had for fifty cents.

Corner Store (1981-1983): Like many storefronts, the second and third stories of the Corner Store had room for the shopkeeper's family or the landlord's mother-in-law.

I n 1982, the Snow Village experienced a design change reminiscent of the one that took place in 1977, when the buildings first began to display increased detail and a wider range of architectural styles. Although any sampling of pieces from various years always fits together in a picturesque grouping, there is no mistaking that after six years, Snow Village design and crafting techniques had developed considerably. Compare the split logs, shuttered windows and railed balcony of the Swiss Chalet to its predecessor, the 1976 Small Chalet. Revolving doors, brimming window boxes, and fan windows added a new dimension to the quaint, simple charm of the 1982 introductions, which included the Skating Pond, Street Car, Centennial House, Carriage House, Pioneer Church, Swiss Chalet, Bank, Gabled House, Flower Shop, New Stone Church, and the Snowman with Broom accessory.

There were three new pieces added this year that, like the 1978 Skating Rink and Duck Pond, or the 1980 Train Station and Train, gave our imaginations a special kind of access to the Snow Village. Starting in 1982, the Street Car, a faded memory in most parts of the world, clanged merrily down Main Street, helping to create an atmosphere of days gone by. The new Skating Pond, this time flanked by two snow-laden trees, was brought back by popular demand following the early retirement of the original Skating Rink/Duck Pond Set after only one year. Last, but certainly not least, the Snowman With Broom, first offered in 1982, holds its place in history both as the longest running accessory piece ever, and the only piece introduced prior to 1985 that is still available today!

In 1982, the Snow Village experienced a design change reminiscent of the one that took place in 1977, when the buildings first began to display increased detail and a wider range of architectural styles. Although any sampling of pieces from various years always fits together in a picturesque grouping, there is no mistaking that after six years, Snow Village design and crafting techniques had developed considerably. Compare the split logs, shuttered windows and railed balcony of the Swiss Chalet to its predecessor, the 1976 Small Chalet. Revolving doors, brimming window boxes, and fan windows added a new dimension to the quaint, simple charm of the 1982 introductions, which included the Skating Pond, Street Car, Centennial House, Carriage House, Pioneer Church, Swiss Chalet, Bank, Gabled House, Flower Shop, New Stone Church, and the Snowman with Broom accessory.

There were three new pieces added this year that, like the 1978 Skating Rink and Duck Pond, or the 1980 Train Station and Train, gave our imaginations a special kind of access to the Snow Village. Starting in 1982, the Street Car, a faded memory in most parts of the world, clanged merrily down Main Street, helping to create an atmosphere of days gone by. The new Skating Pond, this time flanked by two snow-laden trees, was brought back by popular demand following the early retirement of the original Skating Rink/Duck Pond Set after only one year. Last, but certainly not least, the Snowman With Broom, first offered in 1982, holds its place in history both as the longest running accessory piece ever, and the only piece introduced prior to 1985 that is still available today!

Historical Footnote: The brief appearance in 1982 of six light-up tree ornaments became a source of confusion for some Snow Village followers. The ornaments, designed to fit over the miniature tree bulbs, were made of hand painted wood rather than ceramic, and were destined to take their place in history a bit sooner than most Original Snow Village items. The six ornament designs included the Gabled House (1981), the Swiss Chalet (1982), the Countryside Church (1979), the Carriage House (1982), the Pioneer Church (1982), and the Centennial House (1982). Due to extensive production problems, the ornaments were retired almost before they were introduced, and Department 56 has been unable to locate samples or photographs of these unusual Snow Village relatives.

New Stone Church (1982-1984): This last version of the Stone Churches (see 1977, 1979) featured an entirely new design in the same distinctive colors.

Bank (1982-1983): The corner sign, "revolving doors" and attached stairway of the Bank were an outstanding achievement by a clever Snow Village sculptor.

ower Shop (1982-1983): This shop, with greenhouse, utters and bright, rolled awnings, was a good place to stop and hell the flowers.

Street Car (1982-1984): If your desire was a street car, your wish was granted when the bright yellow #2 Street Car line was established in 1982.

wiss Chalet (1982-1984): The Bavarian style of this alpine halet was typical of regions throughout Germany, Austria, vitzerland.

Pioneer Church (1982-1984): Designed to look as if it were constructed entirely of wood, the Pioneer Church was a quaint, rugged structure with a simple message.

Gabled House (1982-1983): Delicate "embroidered" curtains, four gables and two small corner porches added charm to the shingled exterior of this modest house.

Centennial House (1982-1984): This clapboard two-story home, with its tall square tower, mansard roof and wooden porches really looked 100 years old.

Carriage House (1982-1984): The lamps above the big doors at the Carriage House were always lit to welcome the coach driver, who lived in the cozy apartment above.

Skating Pond (1982-1984): Replacing the Skating Rink/Duck Pond Set, this lighted accessory piece was molded in two parts to prevent the heavy trees from breaking loose.

From 1976 to 1982, Department 56 had introduced a total of 49 lit designs (including lit accessory pieces) to The Original Snow Village Collection, retiring a total of 29. In 1983, with the addition of 12 new pieces, there were 32 designs available, the largest offering of lit pieces for a single year in Snow Village history. As the Snow Village grew, our vision of the quiet river valley had to grow with it. As in many small, developing towns, many changes in the landscape occurred over the years, but the scene was no less captivating as a result.

The 1983 introductions reflected the changes that had been gradually overtaking the Snow Village as the tiny township prospered. Government was represented for the first time in the stately Town Hall and Governor's Mansion. Many buildings, including the Turn of the Century, the Gothic Church, and the Parsonage displayed the substantial brick and stone architectural style common in the late nineteenth century. The charming facades of the Fire Station and Grocery, the ornate Victorian Cottage and Chateau, the Village Church, Wooden Church, English Tudor, Gingerbread House and Monks-A-Caroling were further evidence of the transformation of a tiny Snow Village into a bustling boom town.

The one thing that would never change was the idea which had originally inspired the Snow Village. The idea had always been to recreate for everyone warm, joyful holiday feelings sparked by images of a quaint, snow-covered village. The idea is still the same today. We can never be closer to understanding the true meaning of the season than when we recall the beloved memories and traditions that we cherish most. In its eighth year, The Original Snow Village was beginning to do more than just recall for us our favorite holiday memories...it was becoming one.

Grocery (1983-1985): The very charming, detailed Grocery was the only shop design ever issued with fully sculpted, handpainted front display windows.

Chateau (1983-1984): The increased detail in Snow Village design, sculpting, and hand painting was beautifully demonstrated in this European-looking villa.

Governor's Mansion (1983-1985): The lucky governor of the Snow Village occupied this gracious mansion, which featured some of the first metal trim on its front tower.

Victorian Cottage (1983-1984): Fancy gingerbread, involved roof lines, dark coloring, and porch pillars were typical Victorian characteristics of this cottage.

Fire Station (1983-1984): The first Snow Village Fire Station remains one of the most charmingly sculpted pieces in the history of the series.

Parsonage (1983-1985): An old parsonage like this one was usually large and sturdy to withstand the endless charitable needs of the church community.

Town Hall (1983-1984): After seven years of continued growth, The Original Snow Village landscape was governed by the sturdy brick and limestone Town Hall in 1983.

Turn of the Century (1983-1986): The only feature not built to last on this solid-looking house seemed to be the front window shutter on the third floor.

Village Church (1983-1984): In 1983, the whole countryside parish of the Village Church donated their old barn paint for the purpose of beautifying the church roof.

Historical Footnote: For the first time in 1983, the Governor's Mansion and the Gothic Church incorporated molded metal trim into the design of the ceramic buildings. This mixed-media design element eventually became quite charming and elaborate in such pieces as the Home Sweet Home Windmill (1988) and the Water Tower (1988), a non-lit accessory piece.

Historical Footnote: After just one year, the makers of the original 1983 Monks-A-Caroling were unable to supply the item, forcing retirement of this very popular piece. However, another source was soon discovered, allowing an identical set of Monks to continue the caroling in 1984.

Gothic Church (1983-1986): The architectural style for which this church was named is revealed in the sloping roof, pointed arches and ornate grillwork on the steeple.

Historical Footnote: The 1983 Gingerbread House, introduced as a coin bank, was the only non-lit house design ever "constructed" in The Original Snow Village. One of the most charmingly sculpted and handpainted examples ever issued, the Gingerbread House had a single coin slot cut into the roof instead of the traditional window openings featured on the lighted designs. This piece was the only design that could literally become more "valuable" each year!

Gingerbread House (1983-1984): Designed as a coin bank, this sweet model was the only piece ever introduced that was meant to be non-lit. It was also non-edible.

English Tudor (1983-1985): Thick walls kept cottages like this cool in summer, and the winter cold was no match for the fireplaces located throughout the first floor.

Wooden Church (1983-1985): The crossed timbers, side chapel, steeple and front entrance adorning this piece were all separate attachments.

T he hope that the Snow Village would offer something for everyone required that a large number of different styles be incorporated into a relatively small setting. This made it no different than almost any town, large or small. People have always built houses using familiar influences, whether it is a reminder of their homeland, the house in which they grew up, or just a memory of a place that brought comfort and happiness.

The wide selection of houses offered in 1984 represented a sampling of influences from all over the country. The Bayport, typical of the New England coastal area, was just as charming as the Stratford House, a small, tudor-style piece. The airy Summit House, reminiscent of the west coast, stood side by side with the more stalwart Delta and Galena Houses, midwestern from towers to trim. Other designs included the Main Street House, Haversham House, River Road House, and the New School House. Up through 1984, only six accessory items had been offered, including this year's Scottie with Tree and Monks-A-Caroling (see 1983 Historical Footnote, p. 47), but there would soon be a drastic change in the role of Snow Village accessories.

Many styles of churches were offered through the years, patterned after a wide assortment of inspirational buildings. Church designs have always evoked powerful, deeply personal feelings, and the lighted steeples of the Trinity, Parish, and Congregational Churches, introduced in 1984, were excellent examples of traditional churches designed to spread peace and good will.

A grand total of 73 lit pieces had been issued in The Original Snow Village series since 1976, including the 12 new lighted designs introduced in 1984. But the collection was not impressive because of its increasing size and range. It was remarkable because each individual piece represented the same warm, traditional qualities for which the Snow Village was becoming famous.

THE COMPLETE 1984 ORIGINAL SNOW VILLAGE© COLLECTION

Historical Footnote: The brightly colored dots of blue, yellow and red that grace the "curtains" in the Summit House and the Galena House are a traditional Original Snow Village feature dating back to the Victorian House, issued in 1977. These colorful window treatments continue to appear on current designs, such as the Kenwood House, introduced in 1988.

Historical Footnote: The 1984 Congregational Church was the only Snow Village church design ever introduced whose title carried a specified denomination.

Summit House (1984-1985): Looking as i belonged on a sunny California streetcorn the drifts on the Summit House roof reveal its true Snow Village location.

Bayport (1984-1986): This coastal clapboard design was suggestive of the eastern seaboard, but the Snow Village version, protected from the elements, never needed repainting.

Stratford House (1984-1986): The orn mental timbering on the exterior of this sma but elegant home gave it a Dickensian loc that inspired its English name.

New School House (1984-1986): Snow Village kids loved the big, two-story New School House because the clock always read 3 o'clock, and school was permanently "out!"

Trinity Church (1984-1986): Many old churches took years to complete, time during which styles often changed or funds ran out, resulting in asymmetrical architecture.

Haversham House (1984-1987): Colorful brick, balconies, porches, gingerbread and a gabled front tower made the Haversham House a popular design for four years.

Galena House (1984-1985): Galena, Illinois is known for its abundance of fine, well-kept historic homes, a characteristic it shares with The Original Snow Village.

Parish Church (1984-1986): Just a simple country church, this piece required over 200 hand-cuts to create the windows, and featured a multi-story attached steeple.

River Road House (1984-1987): Grand homes like this have graced the nation's river banks since the paddlewheel boats churned their way from St. Paul to New Orleans.

Delta House (1984-1986): Reminiscent of fraternity and sorority communities everywhere, this big, brick university-style house was also a study in attachments.

Main Street House (1984-1986): As the name implied, this typical one-and-a-half story home fit charmingly in every neighborhood, from Sauk Rapids to the Snow Village.

Congregational Church (1984-1985): Its hand painting and hand-cut vented steeple made this small and simple puritan-style church a time consuming piece to produce.

It was "just imagination" which prompted the introduction in 1985 of five accessories that brought a new kind of warmth to the sparsely populated village streets. These accessory pieces began a new era in which The Original Snow Village accessories contributed as much to the atmosphere of the setting as did the houses that had started it all.

Three of these items, each a set of two, reminded us that there is nothing so enchanting as the excitement and wonder displayed by children during the holidays. There was a toboggan loaded with three adorable youngsters braced for a breathless toboggan ride, and an adventurous little girl testing out a brand new pair of skis (Snow Kids Sled/Skis). We could mail a letter to the North Pole with a rosy-cheeked girl, balance on the rooftop with Santa (Santa/Mailbox), step out in the yard to feed some hungry geese, or go holiday shopping with Mother (Family Mom/Kids, Goose/Girl). What these accessories gave us was a key with which we could unlock our imaginations. Their happy faces and familiar holiday activities recalled for us the child-like thrill of the season, brightened up the Snow Village, and helped us to believe, at least for a moment, that we were really there.

The eight lighted pieces introduced in 1985 were almost exclusively residential designs, with just one church and a new Depot and Train with Two Train Cars. The new Depot, a four-piece set with non-lighting train, was the second of three train stations to be introduced, replacing the original Train Station with Three Train Cars. Other building designs featured the classic Williamsburg and Plantation Houses, as well as Spruce Place, Stucco Bungalow, Ridgewood, Duplex, and the Church of the Open Door. Completing the list of accessories were the Singing Nuns and the familiar old favorite, Auto with Tree, which is the only 1985 piece still available today.

Historical Footnote: Many of the Snow Village designs underwent minor changes over the years. Birds changed from blue to red, and sometimes disappeared altogether. Houses underwent alterations in color, window openings and trim. For example, the 1978 General Store was introduced as a white building with a gray roof, but examples have been found with tan siding and a red roof! These differences are all evidence of the many hand-done processes involved in the making of every Snow Village piece. Variations will inevitably occur. When a piece is finished by hand, there will never be two pieces that are exactly alike!

Spruce Place (1985-1987): Snow Village craftsmen had come a long way from the 1977 Victoria House, but the front steps still had to be swept.

Williamsburg House (1985-1988): This traditional two-story Colonial featured three dormers, two chimneys, entry porch and snow-laden tree, all separately attached.

Plantation House (1985-1987): If Scarlett O'Hara had been able to collect this piece from The Original Snow Village, she might never have gone back to Tara.

Church of the Open Door (1985-1988): Several Snow Village church designs featured welcoming front doors that stood ajar, but this particular model ironically did not.

Ridgewood (1985-1987): Imagine spending the holidays in a big frontier-style house like the Ridgewood, where fresh garlands were made from the snow-laden tree out back.

Duplex (1985-1987): Common in the twenties, thirties and forties, the duplex was a two-family dwelling with a common entrance and walls you could easily hear through.

Depot and Train with 2 Train Cars (1985-1988): Altered considerably in size, color and design, the second of three train stations was accompanied by a non-lit train.

Stucco Bungalow (1985-1986): A concrete cousin to the 1984 Main Street House, the Stucco Bungalow added a wreath and garland to enhance the neighborhood holiday spirit.

The largest introduction of lit pieces in Snow Village history occurred in 1986, when 16 new buildings appeared on the scene accompanied by three new accessories. There were ten houses, two churches, a diner and three designs that created the new Main Street "business district."

The 1986 accessories exhibited the child-like innocence first introduced in the 1985 accessory groupings. A tiny twosome added the finishing touches to a roly-poly snowman (Girl/Snowman, Boy), a set of shivering shoppers happily displayed their brightly wrapped gifts (Shopping Girls with Packages), and four little merry-makers frolicked hand-in-hand 'round a snow-laden tree (Kids Around the Tree). Their breathless shouts and excited giggles could be heard echoing throughout the Snow Village and right into our homes.

As in previous years, the house designs reflected a wide range of influences, from the San Francisco-style Pacific Heights House to the Bostonian Beacon Hill and the midwestern Lincoln Park Duplex, Waverly Place, Twin Peaks, and 2101 Maple. The Sonoma, Highland Park, Ramsey Hill and Carriage Houses each had unique personalities, but none could match the ever-popular Diner. The churches, including the classic country-style of the All Saints Church and the sturdy towers of the St. James Church, were welcome additions to the Church of the Open Door, the only church from previous years that had not been retired.

The business district, introduced in 1986, would eventually become the center of the Snow Village as we know it today. In this "downtown" area, the Toy Shop, the Bakery and the Apothecary shops created a charmingly authentic representation of Main Street America. The late nineteenth-century, ornamental brick facades were easily recognized, nostalgic images that instantly affected us in the now familiar tradition of The Original Snow Village. Their warm, small-town feeling reminded us of simpler times, of the peace, hope and goodwill that are the most important, most universal sentiments of the holiday season.

Historical Footnote: Waverly Place, Twin Peaks, and 2101 Maple are listed as designed in the calendar year 1986, and would therefore not be available in stores until the following year, 1987. However, because of an exclusive contract agreement between Department 56 and a retail buying group, these designs were actually available as Original Snow Village pieces in 1986 to a certain group of retail stores. The designs were not generally available in stores until 1987, when they joined the Department 56 line for just one year.

Bakery (1986-Current): On the corner of Main Street stands the old Bakery, a beautiful example of handpainting, from the front awnings right up to the cupcake.

Apothecary (1986-Current): The Apothecary, marked by a tiny mortar and pestle, was originally designed to fit between the Toy Shop and the Bakery.

Diner (1986-1987): The old train car Diner cooked up the charm in short order, with an added bonus: Free Parking. Just imagine the blue-plate specials at a joint like this!

Toy Shop (1986-Current): A playful teddy bear keeps watch over the striped awnings the Toy Shop, one of the first buildings on the current Snow Village Main Street.

Ramsey Hill House (1986-1989): The abundance of detailed handpainting on the 1986 Ramsey Hill added an extra measure of old-fashioned charm to its Victorian design.

St. James Church (1986-1988): Gold highlighted the main cross and entrances of St. James Church, whose massive double towers became a Snow Village landmark in 1986.

Carriage House (1986-1988): The charm of old carrige houses can never be recreated, so many of the structures are made into modern homes, preserving the old-fashioned flavor.

Lincoln Park Duplex (1986-1988): This piece exhibited lots of charm and colorful character, similar to its real-life counterparts in Chicago's Lincoln Park.

2101 Maple (1986-1986): Now a rare piece of Snow Village history, 2101 Maple was introduced as a modest brick home (see Historical Footnote on this page).

All Saints Church (1986-Current): The image of a small country church was captured at its best in the 1986 All Saints Church, a truly classic church design.

Historical Footnote: In 1986, Department 56 published **Snow Village Tradition,** a small hardcover collector's edition that followed The Original Snow Village Collection through its first ten years. The book was one of the first efforts by Department 56 to provide a growing number of collectors with history and information pertaining to the beloved Snow Village series. Filled with charming, handpainted watercolor illustrations, the tiny volume was very well-received, and even the sharpest readers forgave us for the fact that it contained one or two tiny mistakes! Just imagine!

Snow Village Tradition, published in 1986, was a small, beautifully hand-illustrated chronicle of the first ten years of The Original Snow Village.

Beacon Hill House (1986-1988): Bostonians agree that a well-kept rowhouse is a swell place to be, and this one had a second floor balcony for spectacular marathon viewing.

Pacific Heights House (1986-1988): Unlike those inspirational rowhouses in San Francisco's Pacific Heights, the steps on the Snow Village model needed shoveling.

Highland Park House (1986-1988): The gabled charm of the stucco and brick Highland Park House was typical of tudor style homes built in the twenties and thirties.

Waverly Place (1986-1986): Waverly Place, a bright yellow Victorian, had limited exposure (see Historical Footnote, 1986).

Twin Peaks (1986-1986): The double towers of Twin Peaks were destined for early retirement, along with Waverly Place and 2101 Maple (see Historical Footnote, p. 60).

Sonoma House (1986-1988): The Sonoma's unusual Southwestern architecture was reminiscent of many old winery buildings in the northern California hills.

now drifted gently down through the warm glow of the streetlamps lining Main Street. The Taxi Cab waited at the corner, while a Caroling Family sang traditional holiday songs, accompanied by four members of the pint-sized Children in Band. At the St. Anthony Hotel & Post Office, the last of the holiday mail had been bagged up, and Fire Station No. 2 was decorated for the Firemen's Ball. The giant smokestack of the Snow Village Factory was puffing away (though everyone had gone home for the holidays) and the Lighthouse keeper had just finished decorating his beaming tower with wreaths and garlands galore. It was 1987, and the Snow Village offered more detailed buildings and a greater variety of accessories than ever before. Praying Monks and Three Nuns with Songbooks gathered near the Cathedral Church, while Christmas Children and Snow Kids paraded through the village streets. They were as essential to the life of The Original Snow Village as the houses, shops and churches on which the tradition had been built. In addition to the ceramic accessories, there were new streetlamps, picket fences, "For Sale" signs, and park benches.

The buildings themselves were as diverse as ever, the grand Cumberland House side by side with the simple Jefferson School. The big Red Barn was a perfect companion for the classic white Farm House, and the rich blue Springfield House and the bright green and yellow Snow Village Resort Lodge provided extra splashes of color for the lively village scene. As the range of building and accessory designs increased, the Snow Village was moving closer to the vision of a real old-fashioned town, making it all the easier to find ourselves magically walking the snow-covered streets, peering through cheerfully lit shops windows. The Snow Village made everyone, everywhere welcome. Once inside, it was just as easy to reminisce through favorite old holiday memories as it was to make new ones.

Historical Footnote: In 1987, the second in a series of non-ceramic trees was produced for The Original Snow Village. Pictured in the photographs of the 1987 introductions, these flocked "evergreens" were just one of the many different varieties of additional vegetation available for Snow Village landscaping over the next several years (see p. 98). "Spruce" trees, first introduced in 1986, are pictured in the photographs on pages 60-62.

Historical Footnote: All window openings on The Original Snow Village designs are hand-cut, with each pane requiring up to six individual cuts. The Snow Village Resort Lodge pictured on this page has 68 window openings which required over 350 hand-cuts, one of the highest number of any Snow Village design in history.

Cumberland House (1987-Current): A new garland covers the four pillars which support a curved, sloping roof on the very popular, very grand Cumberland House.

Springfield House (1987-Current): The only problem facing owners of the Springfield House is that Santa would never be able to make it down the very narrow stone chimney.

Snow Village Resort Lodge (1987-1989): This 1987 design was reminiscent of the huge airy seaside homes that were built along the New England coast.

Historical Footnote: The figures that inhabit the snowy streets of the Snow Village could never be exactly true to scale because it would require that the pieces be made so tiny, it would be impossible to produce them in earthenware, the traditional Snow Village medium. The positions, facial expressions, clothing detail and colors would all be lost. In 1987, however, an effort was made to bring the scale of the accessories down as far as possible, while still preserving the lively, colorful charm of the pieces. All designs that were available at this time were remodeled to the present scale, and the size now remains consistent for all subsequent designs.

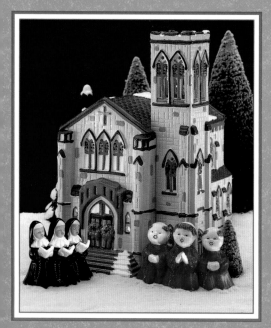

Cathedral Church (1987-Current): One of the largest church designs ever introduced, the Cathedral was the first to feature multi-colored mosaic "stained glass" windows.

Snow Village Factory (1987-1989): Making memories is a tough business, and the Snow Village Factory folded in 1989 after three years of holiday overtime.

Lighthouse (1987-1988): The early retirement of the Lighthouse caused sinking spirits in those who had harbored ideas of collecting, but were afraid to get their feet wet.

Fire Station No. 2 (1987-1989): The live-in firemen at Station No. 2 appreciated the outside stair so they didn't have to climb back up the poles when the fire was out.

St. Anthony Hotel & Post Office (1987-1989): Fourth in a series of Main Street designs, the Hotel was the second design to fly an American flag. The 1979 School House was first.

Jefferson School (1987-Current): This two-room wooden schoolhouse, with its short, square bell tower, represents a typical country school built in the early 1900's.

Farm House (1987-Current): A companion piece for the new Red Barn, the classic white clapboard Farm House even has an old pair of work boots and a butter churn out back.

Red Barn (1987-Current): This second of two barn designs features a hayloft complete with barn cat. The cows, now missing, are out standing in their field.

I n 1988, imaginative new ideas sprang up all over town, resulting in a series of Snow Village "firsts:"

The Village Market, introduced in 1988, was the first of several buildings to incorporate silk-screened "glass" windows, which added a colorful new dimension to the design. It was soon followed by the Corner Cafe and the Cobblestone Antique Shop.

For the first time, the Snow Village offered two designs in 1988 that were interpretations of existing American landmarks, Home Sweet Home and the Maple Ridge Inn.

The other 1988 designs formed a wonderful group of pieces that would compliment any Snow Village setting. The red, white and blue Service Station, with its two ceramic gas pumps, seemed to jump right out of a 1950's gasoline advertisement, and the latest version of the Village Station and Train was reminiscent of every small-town railway station from coast to coast, right down to the bright red soft-drink machine. The Single Car Garage was a natural addition to any collection. A bright red Kenwood House joined the suburban Stonehurst House and the California-style Palos Verdes in the residential section of town. Meanwhile, the stone and mortar Redeemer Church shed its warm, welcoming light throughout the countryside.

Reflecting the growing interest in accessories, fourteen accessory groups were added in 1988, the largest number ever to be introduced in a single year. The new variety of ceramic accessory pieces presented a wealth of opportunity for the Snow Village traveler. A visit to the neighborhood Tree Lot might be followed by a spirited Hayride, a spin in the old Woody Station Wagon, a trip on the big, yellow Schoolbus or a ride on the Snow Plow. There was wood to be chopped (Woodsman and Boy) and garland to be hung (Man on Ladder with Garland). We could pet the dog or rummage through the trash with the family cat (Doghouse/Cat in Garbage Can). Children headed home from school (School Children), or sold apples and newspapers on the streetcorner (Apple Girl/Newspaper Boy), squealing with delight when they saw Santa and eight tiny reindeer Up On A Rooftop!

Redeemer Church (1988-Current): The thickly shingled roof, lancet windows, stone quoins and heavy wooden doors give this country-style church a warm, rustic quality.

Palos Verdes (1988-Current): Originally planned for a Southern California community, this Spanish-style home looks natural enough covered with new-fallen snow.

Stonehurst House (1988-Current): The Stonehurst's three eyebrow dormers, Palladian window, and arched shutters create an unusual but attractive, popular design.

Village Station and Train (1988-Current): The third of three train and station designs, this one typifies the old small town stations which are rapidly disappearing.

Village Market (1988-Current): The new glass windows, first used on the Village Market, allowed light to pass through a silk-screened image rich in color and detail.

Tree Lot (1988-Current): The bulbs hanging from the whitewashed posts and tiny wooden shack of the Tree Lot are traditional signs of the search for a perfect tree.

New metal Fire Hydrants and Mailboxes, stoplights, railroad crossings and a town clock were available (all approved by the Village Council, of course). We could even place a beautiful miniature Nativity in the front yard. Finally, dominating the skyline in 1988 was a new Water Tower proudly displaying the Snow Village name.

Although The Original Snow Village now incorporated some "new-fangled" ideas, its warm, old-fashioned character remained completely intact. A few more details were provided for us, but making the magic journey still depended on our holiday spirit, the strength of our memory and the scope of our imagination.

Kenwood House (1988-Current): The Kenwood's wrap-around porch and imaginative paint job make this charming Queen Anne Victorian a challenge to produce.

Service Station (1988-Current): Big Bill's is a full-service gas station, with a candy machine, restroom, garage, oil rack and ceramic old-time pumps. What, no soda pop?

Single Car Garage (1988-Current): Perfect for any Snow Village lot, the Garage comes with a neat stack of dry firewood, but it's not easy to get the doors open.

Corner Cafe (1988-Current): You know you're in the Snow Village when the cheerful windows of the local cafe advertise twenty-five cent pie and coffee for a nickel.

Cobblestone Antique Shop (1988-Current): Many antique shops like this one actually sell Original Snow Village "antiques," although the series is only fourteen years old.

Maple Ridge Inn (1988-Current): The historic Maple Ridge Inn, a Second Empire Victorian, represents the first Snow Village interpretation of an existing American landmark in upstate New York.

Home Sweet Home/House & Windmill (1988-Current): A classic saltbox and windmill set, this design was based on the original "Home Sweet Home" in East Hampton, New York.

he 1989 introductions emphasized the growing importance of accessory pieces, reflected in the relationship between building and accessory design. The Village Gazebo, with its bright red roof and balustrade, the stars and stripes of the Flag Pole and the dignified Statue of Mark Twain were perfect companion pieces for the long awaited Courthouse. Lively skaters surrounded the Village Warming House as Crack the Whip and Skate Faster, Mom! were introduced. The success of the 1988 Tree Lot inspired Bringing Home the Tree, and a set of rosy-cheeked youngsters carried their Tree Lot selections Through The Woods. Bright red and blue Village Birds were hatched, to perch in the Village Potted Topiary Pair or the Kids' Tree House, and the Choir Kids were designed to file out of every church from 1976 to the present.

The 1989 lighted designs included the bright, nautical blue Jingle Belle Houseboat, docked just upriver from the big wooden waterwheel of J. Young's Granary. "White Christmas", the classic holiday movie, was playing at the Paramount Theater. A gold cross topped the cupola of the very traditional Colonial Church, North Creek Cottage featured the first attached garage, and the sign on the big Victorian Doctor's House guaranteed that the overworked country doctor was always in.

As The Original Snow Village has grown, more and more collectors have suggested items that they would like to see added to the series. In response to a number of requests, the 1989 Street Sign set made it possible for any Snow Village display to feature street names personalized to any particular locale, and a new, two-sided metal For Sale Sign replaced the old model, displaying "For Sale" on one side and "Sold" on the other. The success of the 1988 Woody Station Wagon, School Bus and Snow Plow pieces inspired the Parking Meter and Stop Sign designs. Calling All Cars, featuring a policeman and his squad car, patrolled the area, and Special Delivery, the local postman with his truck, gathered holiday mail from every new Mailbox.

Since 1976, the Snow Village has grown and developed, but as it has grown, it has developed naturally, always remaining faithful to the original idea.

THE COMPLETE 1989 ORIGINAL SNOW VILLAGE© COLLECTION

The feelings associated with the Snow Village have made putting the village together each year a tradition to look forward to, for the joy it can spread to family and friends, and for the special warmth it adds to the holiday season. Those who have spent hours carefully planning know the value of their labor, whether it is for just one favorite piece or one hundred. The anxiously awaited moment arrives when the cords are all tucked in place, the snow is carefully sprinkled, and the tiny lights suddenly spread their welcoming glow throughout a darkened room. It is then that the real magic of The Original Snow Village begins.

Courthouse (1989-Current): Roughly based on the Gibson County Courthouse in Southern India, the Courthouse is typical of many such structures throughout the country.

North Creek Cottage (1989-Current): This Cape Cod cottage, with Colonial front entry porch and sidelights, has a "modern" attached garage to store the family car.

Paramount Theater (1989-Current): The tall, geometric marquee and Spanish-style facade of the Art Deco Paramount Theater are as classic as the movie showing inside.

Doctor's House (1989-Current): The sign says, Doc still makes house calls and the office is in this comfortable old three-story Victorian. Only in the Snow Village!

J. Young's Granary (1989-Current): Down by the old mill stream, J. Young stored grain which could be milled upon request with the help of an old-fashioned waterwheel.

Jingle Belle Houseboat (1989-Current): If you plan to go over the river and through the woods, the Jingle Belle, with her garland, buoy and bell, will get you halfway there.

Village Warming House (1989-Current): A mirror set into the ceramic snow drifts in front of the Warming House created a perfect little "ice" rink, a Snow Village first.

Colonial Church (1989-Current): Typical of Colonial architecture after 1770, this traditional church features a full-height entry porch with four simple Roman columns.

I n 1979, a temporary thaw inspired the introduction of "Meadowland," a small group of pieces featuring a springtime theme. The Thatched Cottage, Countryside Church, Aspen Trees, and Sheep at first received an icy reception from followers of The Original Snow Village, who felt that the softly glowing lights in these pieces lacked the charm provided by a blanket of new-fallen snow. Although the Meadowland pieces are technically not Original Snow Village designs, they have now become treasured additions to many collections because of their very limited distribution. The series was retired in 1980.

What's wrong with this picture? The Meadowland series was not issued as a part of The Original Snow Village because of its springtime theme, but the absence of snow has not deterred avid collectors, many of whom now cherish these very rare pieces.

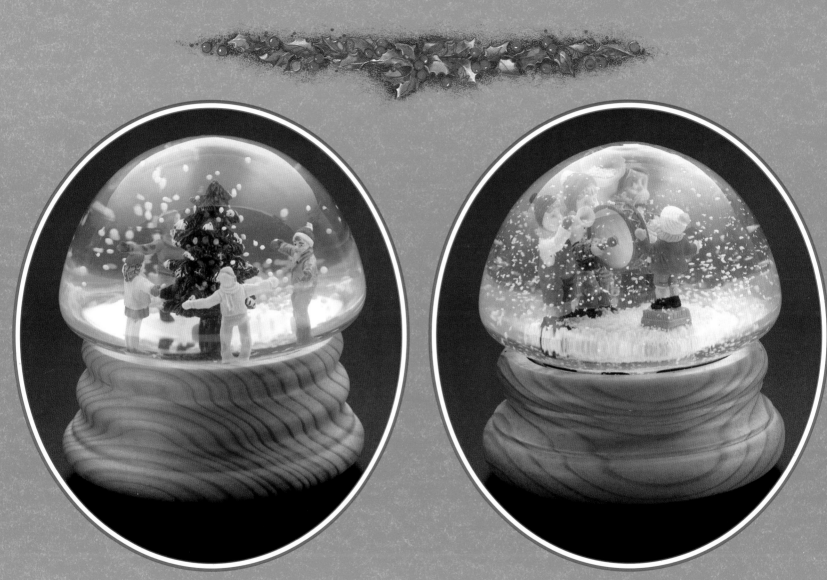

This charming musical waterglobe placed Kids Around the Tree, a popular accessory piece issued in 1986, in the middle of a never-ending snowstorm. The kids didn't seem to mind, and collectors couldn't wait to shake them up.

Both waterglobes introduced in 1988 featured a distinctive mushroom-shaped dome. The Children in Band accessory piece, introduced in 1987, was redesigned for the musical waterglobe pictured above.

Accessories

The first introduction of ceramic accessory pieces occurred in 1979 when the original set of three Carolers started singing beneath their holly-covered lamppost. Since then, accessories have become as important to the growth of The Original Snow Village as the houses, shops and churches which initially inspired this charming holiday tradition. From the simple, early ceramic designs such as Monks-A-Caroling (1983) to the more complicated Crack the Whip (1989), these pieces have caused a lively feeling of holiday activity to spread among the softly glowing lights of the Snow Village.

Over the years, the accessory pieces have developed in much the same way as the lighted ceramic buildings. The Gazebo and Special Delivery demonstrate how improved design, sculpting and handpainting techniques have resulted in pieces that are increasingly more detailed and colorful. Combining ceramic with other materials inspired such classic pieces as Snowman with Broom (1982), Auto with Tree (1985), and the Tree Lot (1988). The availability of new resources and production capabilities brought about exciting new all-metal pieces like the Park Bench (1987), the Fire Hydrant (1988) and the Stop Sign (1989).

This chapter features the entire collection of accessory pieces grouped according to year of introduction. The development and increasing importance of these charming pieces can be traced through the following pages, and it is easy to see that with each succeeding year, the accessories have added a brighter spark of life to the nostalgic tradition of The Original Snow Village.

1979

Carolers (1979-1986): These early carolers, the first sign of life on the village streets, sang faithfully until the 1987 Caroling Family gave them a rest.

1980

Ceramic Car (1980-1986): If you liked old-time roadsters, you were in luck because no other car models were available until 1985.

1981

Ceramic Sleigh (1981-1986): Filled with bright packages and a fresh-cut tree, the Sleigh was a great way to travel, reindeer not included.

1982

Snowman with Broom (1982-Current): The Snowman has been carrying his broom for so long, he's the oldest Original Snow Village piece still available today.

1983

Monks-A-Caroling (1983-1984): These four friendly friars followed the fold faithfully until their identical twin "brothers" took over from 1984-1988.

1984

Scottie with Tree (1984-1985): The ever-popular black Scottie dog waited in vain beside this little tree for the fire hydrants which weren't introduced until 1988.

Singing Nuns (1985-1987): The Singing Nuns were a companion piece to the 1984 Monks-A-Caroling, and both were collected religiously.

Auto with Tree (1985-Current): The oldest piece currently available other than the 1982 Snowman with Broom, this accessory combined a sisal tree with a ceramic car.

Family Mom/Kids, Goose/Girl (1985-1988): The new accessories, far more detailed in design, were also more colorful and realistic than their predecessors.

Santa/Mailbox (1985-1988): Santa finally made an appearance in the Snow Village in 1985, probably as a result of a letter he received from an anxious little girl.

Snow Kids Sled, Skis (1985-1987): A new breed of Snow Village accessories was introduced in 1985 that featured cute characters like these full of lively holiday fun.

1986

Girl/Snowman, Boy (1986-1987): This frosty two-piece group reminded us that no matter how old we are, one of life's simple pleasures is building the perfect snowman.

Kids Around the Tree (1986-Current): The joyous spirit of children joining hands to dance around a holiday tree is just the kind of feeling the Snow Village was created to spread.

Shopping Girls with Packages (1986-1988): Proudly displaying their holiday purchases, these girls were ready to celebrate by opening some gifts of their own.

Christmas Children (1987-Current): The innocent holiday excitement of childhood, captured in pieces like these, has always been a part of The Original Snow Village.

Snow Kids (1987-Current): This grouping incorporates Snow Kids Sled/Skis (1985) and Girl/Snowman, Boy (1986), rescaled to the smaller 1987 size that has become standard.

Children in Band (1987-1989): The complexity of the Children in Band accessory required that each figure be cast separately and treated as an attachment to the base.

Caroling Family (1987-Current): Compared with the 1979 Carolers, this grouping demonstrates the wonderful design and crafting techniques developed over the years.

3 Nuns with Songbooks (1987-1988): Smaller in scale than their retired "sisters," these nuns made a habit of caroling through the Snow Village for two years.

Praying Monks (1987-1988): As simple as this piece looks, it required five different paint colors, including the gold for the crucifixes detailed on the robes.

Taxi Cab (1987-Current): The delightful Taxi design was nearly scrapped due to the difficulty of handpainting the checkerboard pattern, but a decal solved the problem.

For Sale Sign (1987-1989): The holly-covered For Sale Sign was selling Village homes for three years until the redesigned metal sign came on the market in 1989.

Picket Fence (1987-Current): The first metal accessory in The Original Show Village. **Park Bench (1987-Current):** The dark green metal Park Bench was also introduced in 1987.

1988

Up On A Rooftop (1988-Current): And what to your wondering eyes should appear, but a miniature pewter sleigh and eight tiny reindeer! (4″ long from Dasher to Santa)

Fire Hydrant and Mailbox (1988-Current): In smaller scale, ceramic cannot hold detail and is too lightweight, so accessories like these are cast in metal.

Apple Girl/Newspaper Boy (1988-Current): In the Snow Village, apples are still a nickel and newsboys hawk papers on the corner. Some things will never change.

Woodsman and Boy (1988-Current): Increasing detail and an advanced standard of handpainting are evident on this father and son set of two, designed in 1988.

Doghouse/Cat in Garbage Can (1988-Current): As this Snow Village pooch patiently awaits his holiday mail, a feline friend searches for an appropriate gift.

Sisal Tree Lot (1988-Current): This tree lot provided all different tree varieties, as indicated by the signs, but no miniature lights and no traditional shack.

Woody Station Wagon (1988-Current): The Woody is a reminder of days gone by, when everyone travelled for the holidays, but Santa was the only one who could fly.

School Children (1988-Current): When these smart looking students grabbed their books and lunchboxes, the enrollment figure in the Snow Village school system jumped to three.

School Bus, Snow Plow (1988-Current): With all that new-fallen snow, this is the busiest plow in the world, but school is out for the holidays, so the bus is empty.

Man on Ladder with Garland (1988-Current): A wooden ladder, a ceramic figure and a fiber garland, all made in separate locales, are assembled in a single accessory piece.

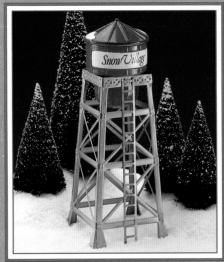

Water Tower (1988-Current): A metal scaffold supports a ceramic "reservoir" on the Water Tower, which proudly displays the Snow Village name.

Hayride (1988-Current): To create this very charming accessory, the horse and sleigh are molded as one unit, and the characters are four separate attachments.

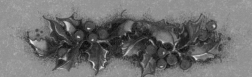

Town Clock (1988-Current): The Town Clock is a charming addition to any Snow Village setting, and on its metal face, as in the imaginary town, time seems frozen.

Tree Lot (1988-Current): The bulbs hanging from the whitewashed posts and tiny wooden shack of the Tree Lot are traditional signs of the search for a perfect tree.

Nativity (1988-Current): This little creche scene, crafted in earthenware and cold-cast porcelain, has become a classic holiday yard ornament in the Snow Village.

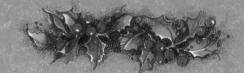

1989

Crack the Whip (1989-Current): This set is an excellent example of the many advances that have been made in the design, molding and handpainting of accessory pieces.

Skate Faster, Mom (1989-Current): The two adorable sleigh riders are as excited as can be to dash across the snowy, slippery ice, but not as breathless as Mom.

Bringing Home the Tree (1989-Current): Combining media on an accessory can give it added life, as on this team carrying out their traditional holiday mission.

Through the Woods (1989-Current): En route to Grandmother's house, these cheerful children carry holiday trim from the Tree Lot, but how did they get over the river?

Statue of Mark Twain (1989-Current): The recently sculpted Statue of Mark Twain is a Snow Village tribute to the creator of some of America's most nostalgic heroes.

Parking Meter (1989-Current): A nickel will park your station wagon anywhere in the Snow Village, but if you don't have any change, most of these have time left on them.

Mailbox (1989-Current): Since the Snow Village is responsible for generating almost half of the letters to Santa, this mailbox accessory is a welcome addition.

Stop Sign (1989-Current): With all the Snow Village traffic lately, these metal Stop Signs have been made available for those who find themselves in a jam.

For Sale Sign (1989-Current): This new For Sale Sign features an enameled metal sign-post, colorful birds and a free-hanging sign which reads "For Sale" or "Sold."

Street Sign (1989-Current): The Snow Village Street Signs offer the ability to enhance a setting with charming street names on labels that can be personalized.

Village Potted Topiary Pair (1989-Current): A sisal topiary tree firmly planted in a traditional base has made formal gardening the pride of the Snow Village.

Calling All Cars (1989-Current): The streets of the Snow Village are so safe, the policemen can't wait to direct traffic when the stoplights go on the blink.

Choir Kids (1989-Current): Following in the footsteps of the retired Monks and Nuns, this cheery young group brings a joyful new noise to the Snow Village.

Village Birds (1989-Current): These tiny, self-perching, metal cuties ended the debate over red birds and blue birds, because both are now readily available.

Special Delivery (1989-Current): As the holidays draw nearer, the mailman and his truck get a workout delivering all the special cards and packages we so anxiously await.

Village Gazebo (1989-Current): The bright red roof of the Gazebo offers shelter from the frequently-falling snow, or a romantic spot to reflect on cherished holiday memories.

Kids Tree House (1989-Current): Now that the tree is decorated, there is an ultra-top-extra-specially secret Christmas meeting going on inside the clubhouse.

Flag Pole (1989-Current): The resin base, metal pole, cloth flag and thread rope make the assembly of this accessory a challenge even Betsy Ross would respect.

ew design and production techniques have allowed the degree of detail in The Original Snow Village ceramic pieces to steadily increase. To compliment this, a new form of accessory was required that could offer a new dimension to the village setting. While photographing the 1987 Snow Village catalog (featuring pieces issued in 1986), a local hobby store provided us with a set of miniature streetlamps to add romance to our photos. This happily provided the inspiration we had been seeking. New lighted trim was designed which created the opportunity to put streetlamps or traffic lights on every corner. Each year, new trim ideas have been introduced to challenge the imagination of seasoned collectors as well as those who are putting out their very first welcome mat.

I n addition to the ceramic snow-laden trees which prospered in The Original Snow Village from 1978 to 1989, a growing list of evergreen vegetation has been offered to complete the landscape in various years. These trees, made of different materials ranging from sisal fiber to plastic, added softness to the Snow Village setting and offered the kind of variety that usually occurs naturally in forests and wooded settlements. Creating wintry valleys, tree-covered ridges and carefully landscaped lots has become a rewarding pastime for many collectors of The Original Snow Village.

The Original
Snow Village©
1976-1990

INDEX

*Year issued indicates the year in which the piece was designed, sculpted, and copyrighted. It is possible these pieces may not be available to the collector until the following calendar year.

1976

ISSUE NAME	ITEM NUMBER	YEAR ISSUED*	YEAR RETIRED	PAGE
◾ MOUNTAIN LODGE	5001-3	1976	1979	18
◾ GABLED COTTAGE	5002-1	1976	1979	18
◾ THE INN	5003-9	1976	1979	18
◾ COUNTRY CHURCH	5004-7	1976	1979	18
◾ STEEPLED CHURCH	5005-4	1976	1979	18
◾ SMALL CHALET	5006-2	1976	1979	18

1977

ISSUE NAME	ITEM NUMBER	YEAR ISSUED*	YEAR RETIRED	PAGE
◾ VICTORIAN HOUSE	5007-0	1977	1979	22
◾ MANSION	5008-8	1977	1979	22
◾ STONE CHURCH	5009-6	1977	1979	22

1978

ISSUE NAME	ITEM NUMBER	YEAR ISSUED*	YEAR RETIRED	PAGE
◾ HOMESTEAD	5011-2	1978	1984	26
◾ GENERAL STORE	5012-0	1978	1980	26
◾ CAPE COD	5013-8	1978	1980	26
◾ NANTUCKET	5014-6	1978	1986	26
◾ SKATING RINK/DUCK POND SET	5015-3	1978	1979	26
◾ SMALL DOUBLE TREES	5016-1	1978	1989	26

1979

ISSUE NAME	ITEM NUMBER	YEAR ISSUED*	YEAR RETIRED	PAGE
■ MEADOWLAND THATCHED COTTAGE	5050-0	1979	1980	79
■ MEADOWLAND COUNTRYSIDE CHURCH	5051-8	1979	1980	79
■ MEADOWLAND ASPEN TREES (ACCESSORY)	5052-6	1979	1980	79
■ MEADOWLAND SHEEP, 9 WHITE, 3 BLACK (ACCESSORY)	5053-4	1979	1980	79
■ VICTORIAN	5054-2	1979	1982	30
■ KNOB HILL	5055-9	1979	1981	30
■ BROWNSTONE	5056-7	1979	1981	30
■ LOG CABIN	5057-5	1979	1981	30
■ COUNTRYSIDE CHURCH	5058-3	1979	1984	30
■ STONE CHURCH	5059-1	1979	1980	30
■ SCHOOL HOUSE	5060-9	1979	1982	30
■ TUDOR HOUSE	5061-7	1979	1981	30
■ MISSION CHURCH	5062-5	1979	1980	30
■ MOBILE HOME	5063-3	1979	1980	30
■ GIANT TREES	5065-8	1979	1982	30
■ ADOBE HOUSE	5066-6	1979	1980	30
■ CAROLERS (ACCESSORY)	5064-1	1979	1986	83

1980

ISSUE NAME	ITEM NUMBER	YEAR ISSUED*	YEAR RETIRED	PAGE
■ CATHEDRAL CHURCH	5067-4	1980	1981	34
■ STONE MILL HOUSE	5068-2	1980	1982	34
■ COLONIAL FARM HOUSE	5070-9	1980	1982	34
■ TOWN CHURCH	5071-7	1980	1982	34
■ TRAIN STATION WITH 3 TRAIN CARS	5085-6	1980	1985	34
■ CERAMIC CAR (ACCESSORY)	5069-0	1980	1986	83

1981

ISSUE NAME	ITEM NUMBER	YEAR ISSUED*	YEAR RETIRED	PAGE
■ WOODEN CLAPBOARD	5072-5	1981	1984	38
■ ENGLISH COTTAGE	5073-3	1981	1982	38
■ BARN	5074-1	1981	1984	38
■ CORNER STORE	5076-8	1981	1983	38

1981 (Continued)

ISSUE NAME	ITEM NUMBER	YEAR ISSUED*	YEAR RETIRED	PAGE
■ BAKERY	5077-6	1981	1983	38
■ ENGLISH CHURCH	5078-4	1981	1982	38
■ LARGE SINGLE TREE	5080-6	1981	1989	38
■ CERAMIC SLEIGH (ACCESSORY)	5079-2	1981	1986	83

1982

ISSUE NAME	ITEM NUMBER	YEAR ISSUED*	YEAR RETIRED	PAGE
■ SKATING POND	5017-2	1982	1984	42
■ STREET CAR	5019-9	1982	1984	42
■ CENTENNIAL HOUSE	5020-2	1982	1984	42
■ CARRIAGE HOUSE	5021-0	1982	1984	42
■ PIONEER CHURCH	5022-9	1982	1984	42
■ SWISS CHALET	5023-7	1982	1984	42
■ BANK	5024-5	1982	1983	42
■ GABLED HOUSE	5081-4	1982	1983	42
■ FLOWER SHOP	5082-2	1982	1983	42
■ NEW STONE CHURCH	5083-0	1982	1984	42
■ SNOWMAN WITH BROOM (ACCESSORY)	5018-0	1982	CURRENT	84

1983

ISSUE NAME	ITEM NUMBER	YEAR ISSUED*	YEAR RETIRED	PAGE
■ TOWN HALL	5000-8	1983	1984	46
■ GROCERY	5001-6	1983	1985	46
■ VICTORIAN COTTAGE	5002-4	1983	1984	46
■ GOVERNOR'S MANSION	5003-2	1983	1985	46
■ TURN OF THE CENTURY	5004-0	1983	1986	46
■ GINGERBREAD HOUSE (BANK NON-LIGHTED)	5025-3	1983	1984	48
■ VILLAGE CHURCH	5026-1	1983	1984	46
■ GOTHIC CHURCH	5028-8	1983	1986	47
■ PARSONAGE	5029-6	1983	1985	46
■ WOODEN CHURCH	5031-8	1983	1985	48
■ FIRE STATION	5032-6	1983	1984	46

1983 (Continued)

ISSUE NAME	ITEM NUMBER	YEAR ISSUED *	YEAR RETIRED	PAGE
■ ENGLISH TUDOR	5033-4	1983	1985	48
■ CHATEAU	5084-9	1983	1984	46
■ MONKS-A-CAROLING (ACCESSORY)	6459-9	1983	1984	84

1984

ISSUE NAME	ITEM NUMBER	YEAR ISSUED *	YEAR RETIRED	PAGE
■ MAIN STREET HOUSE	5005-9	1984	1986	52
■ STRATFORD HOUSE	5007-5	1984	1986	52
■ HAVERSHAM HOUSE	5008-3	1984	1987	52
■ GALENA HOUSE	5009-1	1984	1985	52
■ RIVER ROAD HOUSE	5010-5	1984	1987	52
■ DELTA HOUSE	5012-1	1984	1986	52
■ BAYPORT	5015-6	1984	1986	52
■ CONGREGATIONAL CHURCH	5034-2	1984	1985	52
■ TRINITY CHURCH	5035-0	1984	1986	52
■ SUMMIT HOUSE	5036-9	1984	1985	52
■ NEW SCHOOL HOUSE	5037-7	1984	1986	52
■ PARISH CHURCH	5039-3	1984	1986	52
■ SCOTTIE WITH TREE (ACCESSORY)	5038-5	1984	1985	84
■ MONKS-A-CAROLING (ACCESSORY)	5040-7	1984	1988	84

1985

ISSUE NAME	ITEM NUMBER	YEAR ISSUED *	YEAR RETIRED	PAGE
■ STUCCO BUNGALOW	5045-8	1985	1986	56
■ WILLIAMSBURG HOUSE	5046-6	1985	1988	56
■ PLANTATION HOUSE	5047-4	1985	1987	56
■ CHURCH OF THE OPEN DOOR	5048-2	1985	1988	56
■ SPRUCE PLACE	5049-0	1985	1987	56
■ DUPLEX	5050-4	1985	1987	56
■ DEPOT AND TRAIN WITH 2 TRAIN CARS	5051-2	1985	1988	56
■ RIDGEWOOD	5052-0	1985	1987	56
■ SINGING NUNS (ACCESSORY)	5053-9	1985	1987	85

1985 (Continued)

ISSUE NAME	ITEM NUMBER	YEAR ISSUED *	YEAR RETIRED	PAGE
■ AUTO WITH TREE (ACCESSORY)	5055-5	1985	CURRENT	85
■ SNOW KIDS SLED, SKIS (ACCESSORY)	5056-3	1985	1987	85
■ FAMILY MOM/KIDS, GOOSE/GIRL (ACCESSORY)	5057-1	1985	1988	85
■ SANTA/MAILBOX (ACCESSORY)	5059-8	1985	1988	85

1986

ISSUE NAME	ITEM NUMBER	YEAR ISSUED *	YEAR RETIRED	PAGE
■ WAVERLY PLACE	5041-5	1986	1986	62
■ TWIN PEAKS	5042-3	1986	1986	62
■ 2101 MAPLE	5043-1	1986	1986	60
■ LINCOLN PARK DUPLEX	5060-1	1986	1988	60
■ SONOMA HOUSE	5062-8	1986	1988	62
■ HIGHLAND PARK HOUSE	5063-6	1986	1988	62
■ BEACON HILL HOUSE	5065-2	1986	1988	61
■ PACIFIC HEIGHTS HOUSE	5066-0	1986	1988	61
■ RAMSEY HILL HOUSE	5067-9	1986	1989	60
■ SAINT JAMES CHURCH	5068-7	1986	1988	60
■ ALL SAINTS CHURCH	5070-9	1986	CURRENT	60
■ CARRIAGE HOUSE	5071-7	1986	1988	60
■ TOY SHOP	5073-3	1986	CURRENT	60
■ APOTHECARY	5076-8	1986	CURRENT	60
■ BAKERY	5077-6	1986	CURRENT	60
■ DINER	5078-4	1986	1987	60
■ KIDS AROUND THE TREE (ACCESSORY)	5094-6	1986	CURRENT	86
■ GIRL/SNOWMAN, BOY (ACCESSORY)	5095-4	1986	1987	86
■ SHOPPING GIRLS WITH PACKAGES (ACCESSORY)	5096-2	1986	1988	86

1987

ISSUE NAME	ITEM NUMBER	YEAR ISSUED *	YEAR RETIRED	PAGE
■ ST. ANTHONY HOTEL & POST OFFICE	5006-7	1987	1989	67
■ SNOW VILLAGE FACTORY	5013-0	1987	1989	66
■ CATHEDRAL CHURCH	5019-9	1987	CURRENT	66

1987 (Continued)

ISSUE NAME	ITEM NUMBER	YEAR ISSUED *	YEAR RETIRED	PAGE
■ CUMBERLAND HOUSE	5024-5	1987	CURRENT	66
■ SPRINGFIELD HOUSE	5027-0	1987	CURRENT	66
■ LIGHTHOUSE	5030-0	1987	1988	66
■ RED BARN	5081-4	1987	CURRENT	68
■ JEFFERSON SCHOOL	5082-2	1987	CURRENT	67
■ FARM HOUSE	5089-0	1987	CURRENT	68
■ FIRE STATION NO. 2	5091-1	1987	1989	67
■ SNOW VILLAGE RESORT LODGE	5092-0	1987	1989	66
■ PICKET FENCE (ACCESSORY)	5100-4	1987	CURRENT	88
■ 3 NUNS WITH SONGBOOKS (ACCESSORY)	5102-0	1987	1988	88
■ PRAYING MONKS (ACCESSORY)	5103-9	1987	1988	88
■ CHILDREN IN BAND (ACCESSORY)	5104-7	1987	1989	87
■ CAROLING FAMILY, SET OF 3 (ACCESSORY)	5105-5	1987	CURRENT	88
■ TAXI CAB (ACCESSORY)	5106-3	1987	CURRENT	88
■ CHRISTMAS CHILDREN, SET OF 4 (ACCESSORY)	5107-1	1987	CURRENT	87
■ FOR SALE SIGN (ACCESSORY)	5018-0	1987	CURRENT	88
■ PARK BENCH (ACCESSORY)	5019-8	1987	CURRENT	88
■ SNOW KIDS, SET OF 4 (ACCESSORY)	5113-6	1987	CURRENT	87

1988

ISSUE NAME	ITEM NUMBER	YEAR ISSUED *	YEAR RETIRED	PAGE
■ VILLAGE MARKET	5044-0	1988	CURRENT	72
■ KENWOOD HOUSE	5054-7	1988	CURRENT	72
■ MAPLE RIDGE INN	5121-7	1988	CURRENT	74
■ VILLAGE STATION AND TRAIN	5122-5	1988	CURRENT	72
■ COBBLESTONE ANTIQUE SHOP	5123-3	1988	CURRENT	73
■ CORNER CAFE	5124-1	1988	CURRENT	73
■ SINGLE CAR GARAGE	5125-0	1988	CURRENT	72
■ HOME SWEET HOME/HOUSE & WINDMILL	5126-8	1988	CURRENT	74
■ REDEEMER CHURCH	5127-6	1988	CURRENT	72
■ SERVICE STATION	5128-4	1988	CURRENT	72
■ STONEHURST HOUSE	5140-3	1988	CURRENT	72
■ PALOS VERDES	5141-1	1988	CURRENT	72
■ TOWN CLOCK (ACCESSORY)	5110-1	1988	CURRENT	72

1988 (Continued)

ISSUE NAME	ITEM NUMBER	YEAR ISSUED *	YEAR RETIRED	PAGE
■ MAN ON LADDER WITH GARLAND (ACCESSORY)	5116-0	1988	CURRENT	91
■ HAYRIDE (ACCESSORY)	5117-9	1988	CURRENT	91
■ SCHOOL CHILDREN, SET OF 3 (ACCESSORY)	5118-7	1988	CURRENT	90
■ APPLE GIRL/NEWSPAPER BOY, SET OF 2 (ACCESSORY)	5129-2	1988	CURRENT	89
■ WOODSMAN AND BOY, SET OF 2 (ACCESSORY)	5130-6	1988	CURRENT	89
■ DOGHOUSE/CAT IN GARBAGE CAN, SET OF 2 (ACCESSORY)	5131-4	1988	CURRENT	89
■ FIRE HYDRANT AND MAILBOX, SET OF 2 (ACCESSORY)	5132-2	1988	CURRENT	89
■ WATER TOWER (ACCESSORY)	5133-0	1988	CURRENT	91
■ NATIVITY (ACCESSORY)	5135-7	1988	CURRENT	92
■ WOODY STATION WAGON (ACCESSORY)	5136-5	1988	CURRENT	90
■ SCHOOL BUS, SNOW PLOW, SET OF 2 (ACCESSORY)	5137-3	1988	CURRENT	90
■ TREE LOT (ACCESSORY)	5138-1	1988	CURRENT	92
■ UP ON A ROOF TOP (ACCESSORY)	5139-0	1988	CURRENT	89
■ SISAL TREE LOT (ACCESSORY)	8183-3	1988	CURRENT	90

1989

ISSUE NAME	ITEM NUMBER	YEAR ISSUED *	YEAR RETIRED	PAGE
■ JINGLE BELLE HOUSEBOAT	5114-4	1989	CURRENT	78
■ COLONIAL CHURCH	5119-5	1989	CURRENT	78
■ NORTH CREEK COTTAGE	5120-9	1989	CURRENT	78
■ PARAMOUNT THEATER	5142-0	1989	CURRENT	78
■ DOCTOR'S HOUSE	5143-8	1989	CURRENT	78
■ COURTHOUSE	5144-6	1989	CURRENT	78
■ VILLAGE WARMING HOUSE	5145-4	1989	CURRENT	78
■ J. YOUNG'S GRANARY	5149-7	1989	CURRENT	78
■ VILLAGE GAZEBO (ACCESSORY)	5146-2	1989	CURRENT	96
■ CHOIR KIDS (ACCESSORY)	5147-0	1989	CURRENT	95
■ SPECIAL DELIVERY, SET OF 2 (ACCESSORY)	5148-9	1989	CURRENT	95
■ FOR SALE SIGN (ACCESSORY)	5166-7	1989	CURRENT	94
■ STREET SIGN, SET OF 6 (ACCESSORY)	5167-5	1989	CURRENT	94
■ KIDS TREE HOUSE (ACCESSORY)	5168-3	1989	CURRENT	96
■ BRINGING HOME THE TREE (ACCESSORY)	5169-1	1989	CURRENT	93
■ SKATE FASTER MOM (ACCESSORY)	5170-5	1989	CURRENT	93
■ CRACK THE WHIP, SET OF 3 (ACCESSORY)	5171-3	1989	CURRENT	93

1989 (Continued)

ISSUE NAME	ITEM NUMBER	YEAR ISSUED *	YEAR RETIRED	PAGE
■ THROUGH THE WOODS, SET OF 2 (ACCESSORY)	5172-1	1989	CURRENT	93
■ STATUE OF MARK TWAIN (ACCESSORY)	5173-0	1989	CURRENT	93
■ CALLING ALL CARS, SET OF 2 (ACCESSORY)	5174-8	1989	CURRENT	95
■ STOP SIGN, SET OF 2 (ACCESSORY)	5176-4	1989	CURRENT	94
■ FLAG POLE (ACCESSORY)	5177-2	1989	CURRENT	96
■ PARKING METER, SET OF 4 (ACCESSORY)	5178-0	1989	CURRENT	94
■ MAILBOX (ACCESSORY)	5179-9	1989	CURRENT	94
■ VILLAGE BIRDS, SET OF 6 (ACCESSORY)	5180-2	1989	CURRENT	95
■ VILLAGE POTTED TOPIARY PAIR (ACCESSORY)	5192-6	1989	CURRENT	94

Future Village Additions

ISSUE NAME	ITEM NUMBER	YEAR ISSUED *	YEAR RETIRED	RECEIVED FROM

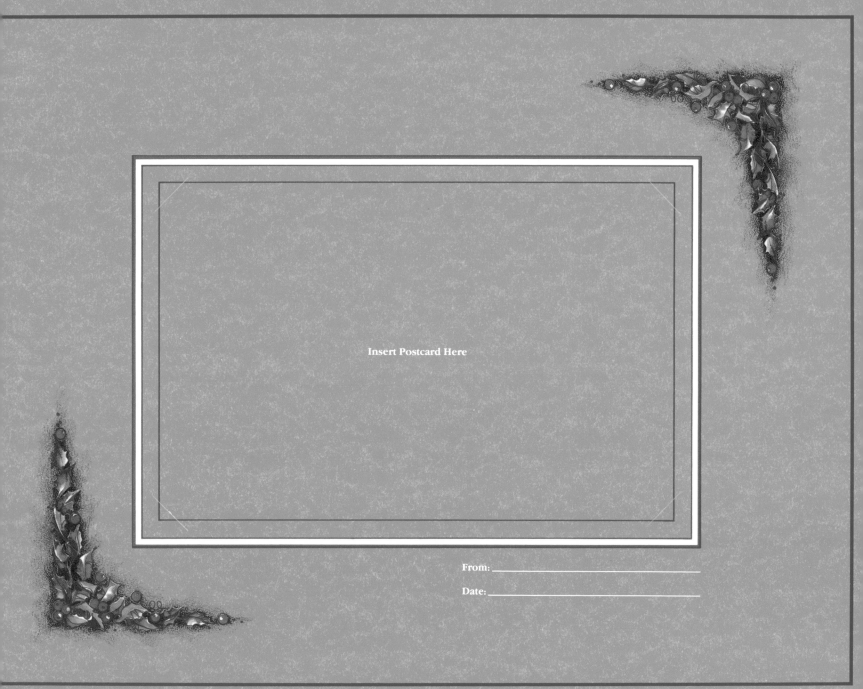

Insert Postcard Here

From: _____

Date: _____

Insert Postcard Here

From: _____

Date: _____

Insert Postcard Here

From: _____

Date: _____

Insert Postcard Here

From: _____

Date: _____

Insert Postcard Here

From: _____

Date: _____

Insert Postcard Here

From: _____

Date: _____

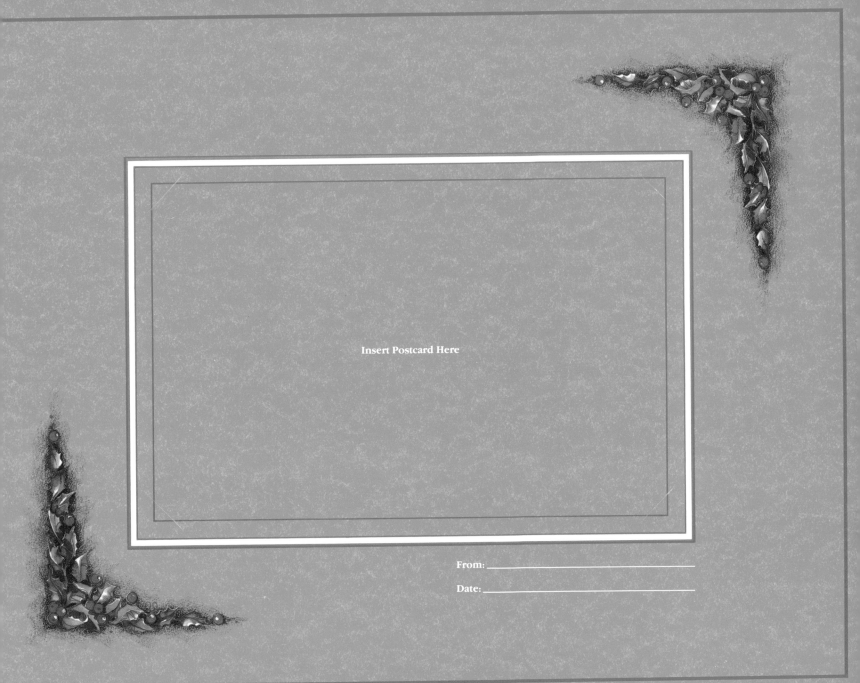

Insert Postcard Here

From: _____

Date: _____

Insert Postcard Here

From: _____

Date: _____

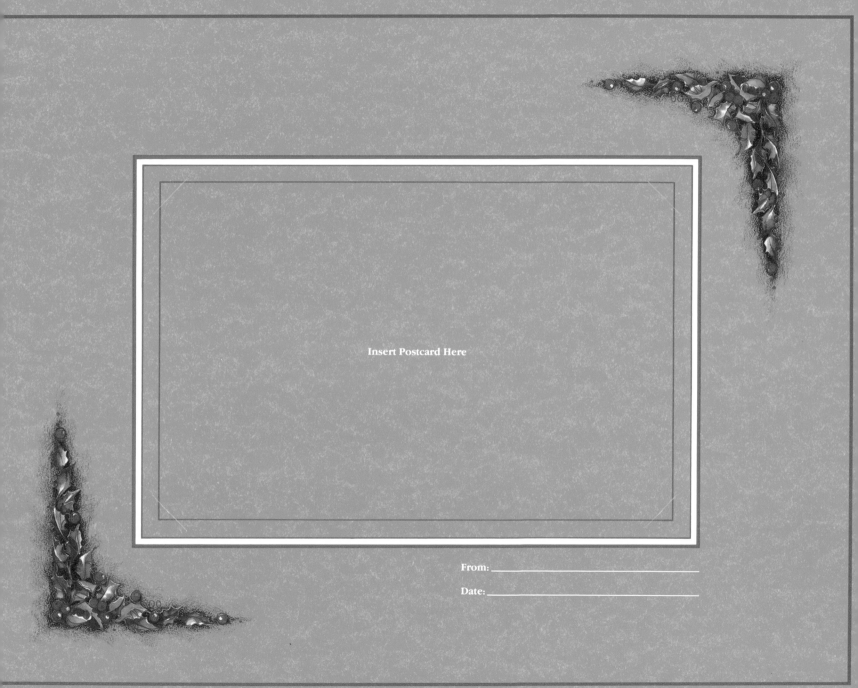

Insert Postcard Here

From: _____

Date: _____

Insert Postcard Here

From: _____

Date: _____

Season's Greetings

Happy Holidays

The **Gabled Cottage** and the **Country Church** from the 1976 Original Snow Village Collection.

The **Nantucket** from the 1978 Original Snow Village Collection.

eason's Greetings

Happy Holidays

The **Town Church** from the 1980 Original
Snow Village Collection.

The **English Cottage** and the **Barn** from the
1981 Original Snow Village Collection.

eason's Greetings

Happy Holidays

The **Parish Church** from the 1984 Original
Snow Village Collection.

The **J. Young's Granary** and the **Village
Warming House** from the 1989 Original
Snow Village Collection.